AF126394

BOOK ANALYSIS

By Verity Roat

The Hate U Give

BY ANGIE THOMAS

BOOK ANALYSIS

Bright
≡Summaries.com

BOOK ANALYSIS

Fifty Shades
of Grey Trilogy
BY E.L. JAMES

Shed new light
on your favorite books with

Bright
≡Summaries.com

www.brightsummaries.com

ANGIE THOMAS

AMERICAN NOVELIST

- **Born in Jackson, Mississippi (U.S.A.) in 1988.**
- **Notable works:**
  - *On the Come Up* (2019), novel

Angie Thomas was born in Jackson, Mississippi, where she witnessed a shootout at the age of six. The next day her mother took her to the library to show her that there was hope in the world. Thomas cites this moment as her inspiration to start writing. She went on to earn a BFA from Belhaven University, where she was the first black student to graduate in creative writing. As a student, Thomas saw the shooting of Oscar Grant (a young African-American man who was shot by police) in the news and this became a major influence on her first novel, *The Hate U Give.* Thomas cites Tupac Shakur (American rapper, 1971-1996) as one of her sources of inspiration – in fact, the title of *The Hate U Give* was taken from his THUG LIFE tattoo, which is an acronym for 'the hate u give little infants fucks everyone'.

Thomas originally gravitated towards fantasy novels, but a college professor suggested that her experiences were unique and that her work could give a voice to people in her community who had been silenced.

THE HATE U GIVE

A YOUNG ADULT CALL TO ACTION AGAINST POLICE BRUTALITY

- **Genre:** novel
- **Reference edition:** Thomas, A. (2017) *The Hate U Give*. [eBook]. London: Walker Books.
- **1st edition:** 2017
- **Themes:** racism, identity, infidelity, gang and drug culture, police brutality, community, the cycle of poverty and crime

As a college student, Angie Thomas was horrified when she heard about the shooting of Oscar Grant in 2009. She reacted to this news by beginning to write the story that would become *The Hate U Give.* It began as a short story for her senior project, but it quickly expanded. After college, she set the project aside to work at her local newspaper, but after hearing about further wrongful shootings and imprisonments in African-American communities across the United States of America, she resumed writing *The Hate U Give.* The novel centres around the unjust shooting of a young African-American man, Khalil, and how his community reacts, with particular focus on the reaction of his childhood friend, Starr, who was with him at the time of his death. Despite Thomas's initial concerns that publishers might not like the Black Lives Matter-inspired subject, the novel has generally been well received.

SUMMARY

THE PARTY

The Hate U Give opens with 16-year-old Starr Carter, narrator and protagonist of the novel, reluctantly attending a party in Garden Heights (the area where she lives, which is mostly populated by the black community) with her friend Kenya. As well as being friends, Kenya and Starr share an older half-brother, Seven. At the party, Starr bumps into her childhood friend and crush, Khalil, who offers to drive Starr home when shots are fired at the party.

On the way home, a police officer, whom Starr later names One-Fifteen (his badge number) pulls Khalil's car over and orders him out of the car. One-Fifteen orders Khalil to stay still while he returns to the patrol car, but Khalil goes to open the door to check on Starr. One-Fifteen shoots Khalil and then points his gun at Starr, telling her not to move until backup and an ambulance arrive.

SECRECY

The following week, Starr returns to Williamson Prep, a private school in a predominantly white area, and decides not to tell anyone that she witnessed Khalil's murder. By this time, Khalil's photo has been plastered all over the news, with him being portrayed as a drug dealer and gang member in order to justify One-Fifteen's actions. Things are especially tense between Starr and her friend Hailey, who unfollowed her Tumblr after she posted a photo of Emmett Till (a young African-American man who was lynched in Mississippi in 1955). Fuelled by concern over Starr's erratic behaviour, Hailey and their mutual friend Maya ask Starr if she knew Khalil, which she denies. She also refuses to explain why she is upset to her white boyfriend, Chris, who also attends Williamson Prep.

THE FUNERAL

Starr attends Khalil's funeral and meets April Ofrah, who is a member of Just Us for Justice, an organisation which seeks to hold police accountable for their actions in cases such as

Khalil's. She tells the congregation at the church that Khalil was unarmed at the time of his death. Kenya's father, King, a notorious gang banger, arrives at the funeral and places a grey bandana on his casket, signifying that he was a King Lord (member of King's gang). This appals Starr, as she is unable to believe that Khalil was involved with drugs and gangs.

AFTERMATH

On the evening of Khalil's funeral, riots begin breaking out in Garden Heights in protest, as the police have announced they will not arrest One-Fifteen and mentioned an unnamed witness. Starr's father, Maverick, goes to protect the local store he owns with Starr, where they find DeVante, a young King Lord who is hiding from King. Maverick offers to help DeVante, as he used to be a King Lord and managed to leave the gang by pleading guilty to a crime which King committed. Maverick asks his brother-in-law, Carlos, to take him in, as Carlos lives outside of Garden Heights.

Meanwhile, Starr learns that Khalil's case is going to be presented before the Grand Jury and agrees to meet with April Ofrah, who persuades her to speak at the trial. Starr learns that One-Fifteen's defence is that he mistook a hairbrush in Khalil's car for a gun. Starr then visits Maya's house with Hailey, where the three of them watch an interview with One-Fifteen's father on television. When Hailey expresses sympathy with One-Fifteen, Starr becomes angry and Hailey storms out. Maya, who is of Chinese heritage, admits that Hailey has also been racist to her in the past. Maya and Starr form a 'minority alliance' and agree to hold Hailey accountable for her actions.

MEDIA AND THE GRAND JURY

Urged on by April Ofrah, Starr gives an anonymous interview with a major TV network, explaining that the media has lied about Khalil and what happened to him. At prom, Chris admits he knows that Starr is the witness, as he recognised her voice, and she feels more able to open up to him about her life in Garden Heights. Because Starr 'dry snitched' (covertly told secrets) about King's status as a gang and drug lord, a brick is thrown through the Carters' window the night before the trial, causing Maverick to seek protection from his former gang mates. The next day,

Starr gives her testimony about what happened to Khalil in front of the grand jury.

VERDICT

After all the negativity they have experienced, Carlos decides to hold a barbecue to celebrate Seven's birthday and graduation to cheer everyone up. His mother, Iesha, turns up uninvited and tells Starr that she needs to be careful, because King (who is Iesha's lover) has had it in for her ever since she snitched on him. Later that night, DeVante disappears and when Starr, Chris and Seven find him, they realise he has been beaten up by the King Lords. Iesha distracts King so that DeVante can escape, even though she knows he will beat her for it.

The grand jury decides not to indict One-Fifteen, causing further riots to erupt in Garden Heights. When his store is set on fire, Maverick finally decides that it is time for the family to move to a safer area, despite his previous protestations that you need to remain in a community in order to be able to help it. DeVante decides to go to the police to provide a witness against King under the promise that he will be locked up for good.

The novel ends with the Carter family happily settled in their new house in a new neighbourhood and Maverick returning to his store with hopes of rebuilding it. The store owner next door offers Maverick his property too so that he can expand and Starr resolves to keep standing up to injustice.

CHARACTER STUDY

STARR CARTER

Starr Carter is a 16-year-old black girl living in Garden Heights. She is both the narrator and protagonist of the novel. Despite living in a poor area, her parents send her to a private school, Williamson Prep, where most of her friends are white. This causes her to feel as though her identity is split into two – 'Garden Heights Starr' and 'Williamson Starr' – and causes her a lot of worry. This is especially prominent in her relationships with her white friends and her white boyfriend; before Khalil's death, she was worried about her dad's reaction to her relationship with Chris and so kept it a secret. After his death, she finds herself called to question her relationship with Chris on a wider level, as well as her friendships with Maya and Hailey. This eventually leads to Starr realise that Hailey often makes racist statements and that she cannot forgive her for this behaviour if she refuses to apologise. Immediately after witnessing Khalil's death, she feels unable to speak out, despite this being the second wrongful shooting she has witnessed (she saw her friend Natasha murdered when she was 10 years old). However, as the book progresses, Starr grows in confidence and eventually vows to always speak out against racism and social injustice.

KHALIL HARRIS

Although he is only briefly present in the novel, Khalil plays an integral role in the narrative of *The Hate U Give.* Khalil is Starr's childhood friend and sweetheart, but they have drifted apart in recent years. Nonetheless, when they bump into each other at a Garden Heights party, they quickly reconnect. When Khalil is shot by a police officer (One-Fifteen) as the two return from the aforementioned party, the injustice of his death forces Starr to reassess her values, friendships and relationships and to speak up against injustice. To begin with, Starr is dismayed when she thinks that Khalil was a gang banger and a drug dealer, but DeVante later reveals that Khalil only sold drugs to pay off his mother's debt to King and that he had actually refused to join the King Lords.

MAVERICK CARTER

Maverick is the father of Seven (with Iesha), Starr and Sekani (with Lisa). He was a member of the King Lords in his youth, but managed to get out of the gang when Starr was little by agreeing to plead guilty to a crime which King committed. During this time, Lisa's brother, Carlos, became a father figure for Starr. His son, Seven, is the result of a one night stand with Iesha when Maverick and Lisa had an argument. Maverick is deeply passionate about improving life in Garden Heights for the whole community.

SEVEN

Seven, Maverick's son by Iesha, is Starr's older brother of whom she says:

> "It's no secret that my big brother is the result of a "for hire" session Daddy had with Iesha after a fight with Momma. Iesha was King's girl, but he told her to "hook Maverick up," not knowing Seven would come along looking exactly like Daddy. Fucked up, I know." (p. 221)

He is unhappy about Iesha's relationship with King and so spends a lot of time at Maverick's house. He attends Williamson Prep with Starr and is fiercely protective of her and his other half-sister, Kenya (Iesha and King's daughter). He has a strained relationship with his mother, but at the end of the novel, wants to forgo college to stay in Garden Heights to protect his mother and sisters, Kenya and Lyric, from King. Maverick, however, tells him not to waste the opportunities given to him and says he will keep an eye on Iesha and her daughters.

KENYA

Kenya is the attractive younger half-sister of Seven and daughter of Iesha and King. She also has a younger sister, Lyric. She is also Starr's best friend and persuades her to go to the party where Starr reconnects with Khalil. Despite their close friendship, Kenya often upsets Starr by referring to Seven as *'my* brother' instead of *'our* brother'. She also berates Starr for forgetting about Garden Heights in favour of her life at Williamson Prep.

CHRIS

Starr's boyfriend who is a white, wealthy student at Williamson Prep. He occasionally makes ignorant comments about race, but he is very supportive of Starr and wants to be a part of all of her life, including Garden Heights.

HAILEY

One of Starr's white friends at Williamson Prep. The two eventually fall out, as Hailey often makes blatantly racist comments which Starr finds hard to cope with after Khalil's death.

MAYA

Starr's friend at Williamson Prep, who is of Chinese origin. Towards the end of the novel, the two form a 'minority alliance' and agree to call out Hailey when she makes racist comments.

UNCLE CARLOS

Starr's maternal uncle, who is also a policeman. He is initially defensive of One-Fifteen's actions, but soon changes his mind and even offers to take in DeVante when he is in trouble. When Maverick was in prison, he became something of a father figure to Starr.

DEVANTE

An adolescent member of King's gang, the King Lords. During the first set of riots, he hides in Maverick's store and asks him to help him to escape from the King Lords. At the end of the novel, he decides to tell the police about King in the hope that he will be put in prison for life.

ONE-FIFTEEN

The policeman who pulls Khalil and Starr over after the party and shoots Khalil. After this incident, he does not appear in person in the novel again.

ANALYSIS

RACE

As the main plotline of *The Hate U Give* centres on the wrongful shooting of Khalil Harris, a young black man, it is unsurprising that race is one of the key themes in the novel. In fact, Thomas said in an interview: "It's funny, because I tell people: "Mississippi is known for two things: writing and racism. And I happen to be a writer who writes about racism" (Lewis, 2019). This gives an indication of how important racism was to her in writing this book. The issue of race manifests itself in several different ways throughout the book.

Systemic racism

The most obvious form is systemic racism, which is explored through Khalil's narrative. As previously stated, Thomas was appalled by the shooting of Oscar Grant, a young black man, and then became deeply interested in the number of similar cases that arose in the following years. As

Starr says in *The Hate U Give*: "I've seen it happen over and over again: a black person gets killed just for being black, and all hell breaks loose" (p. 65), thus indicating that this is a self-perpetuating problem of which her community is aware and which they are fighting to end. From the start, it is clear to the reader that Khalil's death is unjust; he was unarmed, he had committed no crime and when he was pulled over by the policeman, he even told Starr to comply with anything the policeman wanted. The latter shows the scope of this systemic racism; Khalil was expecting unfair treatment from the police and wanted to protect Starr from it. Nonetheless, he is shot by One-Fifteen, who presumes he must be armed on the basis of his race.

This racist perception of Khalil is then furthered by the media within the novel, who portray Khalil as a gang member and drug dealer. While the latter is true, as we find out later in the novel, Khalil had justifiable and noble reasons for doing so and had not been dealing drugs on the night that he was pulled over. Nonetheless, the public then react more sympathetically towards One-Fifteen, whose father says he just wanted to help the community. Even Starr's friends at Williamson Prep express the belief that the world is better off with Khalil dead, as it means one less gang banger in the world.

Starr is horrified by the scope of this systemic racism and seems to be even more infuriated when the racism manifests itself as a somewhat patronising need to help minorities. When One-Fifteen's father states his son wanted to help the community, Starr says: "Funny. Slave masters thought they were making a difference in black people's lives too" (p. 419), thus highlighting the hypocrisy of people like One-Fifteen who profess that they want to help minorities, but still have racist prejudices. This ultimately pushes Starr to speak out about Khalil's death and to fight for justice.

Reverse racism

What is perhaps most interesting and novel about *The Hate U Give* is that Thomas honestly portrays the existence of reverse racism within minority groups. This is most prominently explored in Starr's relationship with Chris: "I can't get the guts to tell Daddy though. And it's not just because he doesn't want me dating yet. The bigger issue is that Chris is white" (p. 78). Starr's fear that her father will disapprove of her relationship with Chris shows that, to some extent, racism has begun to work both ways within black communities. Years of ingrained racism has led older generations in particular to distrust white people. When Starr eventually tells her father about her relationship with Chris, he is initially very upset, but by the end of the novel, his anger has subdued to an extent.

IDENTITY

Starr's life is split into two very distinct parts: the part she shares with her family in Garden Heights and the part she shares with her friends at Williamson Prep. As such, she often feels that her identity has been divided into two and this causes her a great deal of anguish: "I should be used to my two worlds colliding, but I never know which Starr I should be" (p. 576). This confusion over her identity is a recurrent theme throughout the novel. Starr compares it to "flipping the switch" (p. 126) which suggests that, while she finds splitting her personality upsetting, it is something she has control over.

Starr's sense of identity (and her understanding of others' identities) is closely linked to racial factors. For example, she bemoans the fact that her black friends do not think she is cool, saying:

> "The ironic thing is though, at Williamson I don't have to "play it cool" – I'm cool by default because I'm one of the only black kids there. I have to earn coolness in Garden Heights, and that's more difficult than buying retro Jordans on release day." (p. 27)

Starr's opinion of the difference in her 'coolness' at Williamson Prep and in Garden Heights indicates to the author that her identity is intrinsically linked to her race. At Williamson Prep, she is black, which affords her a natural 'coolness', but, in Garden Heights, she is lives in a black community and, as such, her race does not automatically make her 'cool'. On the other hand, there are times when she feels that her race does not benefit her at Williamson Prep; firstly, she experiences casual racism on an almost daily basis from Hailey, who is supposed to be her friend, and secondly, there are certain 'traits', commonly associated with black communities, which Starr hides from her friends at Williamson for fear of alienation. An example of this is the use of slang:

> "Williamson Starr doesn't use slang – if a rapper would say it, she doesn't say it, even if her white friends do. Slang makes them cool. Slang makes her "hood." Williamson Starr holds her tongue when people piss her off so nobody will think she's the "angry black girl." Williamson Starr is approachable. No stank-eyes, side-eyes, none of that. Williamson Starr is nonconfrontational. Basically, Williamson Starr doesn't give anyone a reason to call her ghetto." (p. 126)

Through this exploration of identity, it could be inferred that Thomas is highlighting the hypocritical way that a predominantly white community treats black people. Starr feels she has to carefully choose which aspects of her personality she shows to her white friends at Williamson for fear of appearing too 'black'. This is despite Starr believing that being black automatically makes her 'cool'; perhaps Thomas is suggesting that society dictates there is an optimum 'blackness' which black people feel they must conform to.

This dichotomy is also experienced by Carlos, Starr's uncle. When Khalil dies, Carlos finds himself trapped between two identities: his identity as a policeman and his identity as a black man. Initially, he feels the need to defend One-

Fifteen's actions as a colleague, but eventually he denounces One-Fifteen and feels ashamed for having supported him. As such, we can see that identity is a major issue for the characters in *The Hate U Give*; they often feel torn between two different worlds and it can be very difficult for them to know which side to choose.

FURTHER REFLECTION

SOME QUESTIONS TO THINK ABOUT...

- Teenage friendships feature heavily in *The Hate U Give* and Thomas explores how they intersect with social media. Consider when Starr complains that Hailey has 'unfollowed' her on Tumblr: "Unfollowing me is the same as saying "I don't like you anymore" (p. 137). What role do you think social media plays in teenage relationships today? How does Thomas depict this?
- Compare *The Hate U Give* to *The Fault in Our Stars* (2012) by John Green (American novelist, born in 1977). How do the portrayals of the death of a teenager differ in these two novels?
- Race is a central theme in *The Hate U Give*. How do you think the narrative of this novel would have been different if Khalil had been white?
- Family and community play a large role in *The Hate U Give*. Consider how Thomas depicts these relationships, with particular reference

to Mrs Rosalie (Khalil's grandmother, who looked after Lisa, Starr's mother, when she was a child).

- In *The Hate U Give,* Starr engages in social activism in the hopes of achieving justice for Khalil. Unfortunately, her witness statement to the grand jury does not result in One-Fifteen's conviction. Therefore, do you think Thomas's portrayal of social activism is a positive one or a negative one?

- Why do you think Thomas chose to refer to the officer who killed Khalil as 'One-Fifteen' throughout the novel? What affect does this have on the reader's perception of him?

- What do you think motivates Carlos, Starr's uncle, to take in DeVante, a young King Lord?

- Do you think *The Hate U Give* would have enjoyed the same reception if it had been written ten years previously? Or 50 years previously? Answer with reference to social and cultural factors.

- Examine this quote: "I should be used to my two worlds colliding, but I never know which Starr I should be" (p. 576). What does this tell us about Starr's sense of identity?

We want to hear from you!
Leave a comment on your online library
and share your favourite books on social media!

FURTHER READING

REFERENCE EDITION

- Thomas, A. (2017) *The Hate U Give.* [eBook].
  London: Walker Books.

REFERENCE STUDIES

- Lewis, T. (2019) Angie Thomas, author of The Hate
  U Give: 'Books play a huge part in resistance'.
  The Guardian. [Accessed 5 February 2019].
  Available from: <https://www.theguardian.com/
  books/2019/jan/27/angie-thomas-the-hate-u-give-
  interview-famous-fans-readers>

ADAPTATIONS

- *The Hate U Give.* (2018) [Film]. George Tillman Jr.
  Dir. USA: Fox 2000 Pictures.

BOOK ANALYSIS

Bright ≡Summaries.com

More guides to rediscover your love of literature

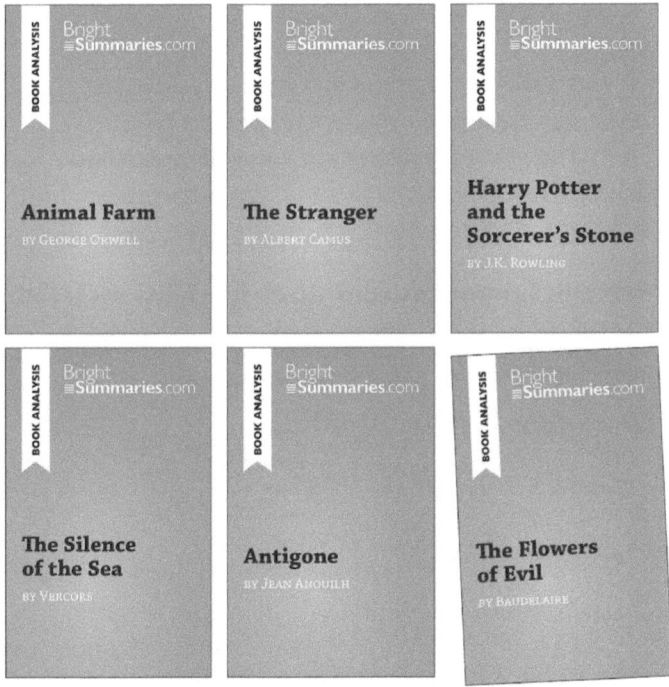

www.brightsummaries.com

Although the editor makes every effort to verify the accuracy of the information published, BrightSummaries.com accepts no responsibility for the content of this book.

© BrightSummaries.com, 2019. All rights reserved.

www.brightsummaries.com

Ebook EAN: 9782808018401

Paperback EAN: 9782808018418

Legal Deposit: D/2019/12603/87

Cover: © Primento

Digital conception by Primento, the digital partner of publishers.